Come to the Stable

A Christmas Musical

Derek Haylock

National Society/Church House Publishing

National Society/Church House Publishing
Church House,
Great Smith Street,
London
SW1P 3NZ

ISBN 0 7151 4840 0

First published in 1994 by The National Society and Church House Publishing

© Derek Haylock 1994

The right of Derek Haylock to be identified as the author of this work has been asserted by him in accordance with the Copyright, Designs and Patents Act 1988.

Performing Rights

Performance of any material in this book, other than in a purely domestic setting, without written permission of the publishers is an infringement of copyright.

Permission for performances by school or Church groups before live, non-paying audiences or live audiences making donations or live paying audiences if the proceeds from ticket sales go to charity will usually be granted without charge provided written permission has been obtained from the publishers prior to performance.

Any professional company wishing to perform the material or any company wishing to do so before a paying audience should apply to the publishers for permission, for which a charge may be made.

The above does not confirm any right to perform any of the material in this book on radio, television, film, video or audio recording, or in any other way except as stated above. Any group wishing to do this must contact the publishers in writing.

Photocopying

Reproduction or transmission in any form or by any means, electronic or mechanical, including photocopy, or use with any information storage or retrieval system, is forbidden without permission in writing from the publisher.

Text design and typesetting by The National Society and Karl Scotland

Cover design by Leigh Hurlock

Printed in Scotland by Indeprint Print Production Services

Scripture quotations are taken from the Holy Bible, New International Version © 1973, 1978, 1984 by International Bible Society. Used by permission of Hodder & Stoughton Ltd. All rights reserved. 'NIV' is a registered trademark of International Bible Society. UK Trademark number 1448790.

Contents

Drama scripts, lyrics and Bible readings
- Version 1 3
- Version 2 20
- Version 3 22

Music
1. Silently down to this world 23
2. Busy at Christmas 24
3. Here in the manger 31
4. The shepherds' shuffle 33
5. March of the wise men 36
6. High on a hillside 39
7. Herod the terror 42
8. All of God's creatures can celebrate . . 46
9. Come to the stable 49
10. If we had a bell 54

Introduction

Come to the Stable is a Christmas musical written with performance mainly by young people in mind, although it would be very appropriate (but not essential) for many of the songs to be supported by an adult choir. The songs, bound together at the end of this book, are arranged here for piano accompaniment. It is hoped that individual musical directors will arrange their own additional instrumental parts to suit their local resources. For rehearsal purposes, for those not reading music, copies of the words of the songs are available for purchase separately.

This musical can be presented in three versions, depending on the availability of resources and the requirements of the groups concerned:

- Version 1 is the full-scale musical, with ten songs, incorporating a drama script for a modern-day family providing a setting for the acting-out in costume of aspects of the story of the first Christmas on-stage. The full version takes about 65 minutes to perform.

- Version 2 is a simpler version which drops the drama script for the modern-day family and omits one of the songs, but retains the acting-out of the story of the first Christmas, with Bible readings used to link the action and songs. Performance time for this version is about 50 minutes.

- Version 3 is simply a series of nine songs linked by Bible readings, with no acting involved. This version also takes about 50 minutes and would be an appropriate format for an adult choir wishing to make use of the material provided here.

Some groups may wish to extract individual songs from the collection provided here for incorporation into their own Christmas programme. Each of the songs stands alone, unconnected by text or musical links to the other songs, and has been written with this possibility in mind.

Derek Haylock
Norwich, February 1994

Version 1

In this full-scale version of the musical, it is envisaged that most of the acting is done by young people. Three areas are required for the performers:

- a central area representing Bethlehem, where the events of the first Christmas are enacted;
- an area to one side, where the modern-day family are situated;
- an area for the choir.

The choir sings some of the songs and lends support to some of the singing by those involved in the action. This could be an adult choir, or a young people's choir, or, preferably, a combination of the two. There is the possibility of four-part singing in the opening and closing songs, although this is not essential. The youngsters playing various parts in the first Christmas story should, of course, be in costume. There is no reason why they should not also form part of the choir when not involved in the action.

The full text of the songs is incorporated into the script which follows, in order to show how the action involving both the modern-day family and the first Christmas fits in with the words of the songs.

The action moves alternately between the modern-day family and the events of the first Christmas. It is most effective if the audience's attention is directed from one to the other by lighting. Alternatively, this could be done by the actors freezing as the scene shifts.

CAST

Modern-day family Mum
Sarah (sullen teenage daughter)
Tom and Anna (two younger children)
Uncle Z
(The composition of the family in terms of males and females can obviously be varied to suit the acting talent available.)

First Christmas Mary and Joseph
Crowd of Citizens in Bethlehem
Group of Census Officers
Group of Shepherds (at least five)
Three Wise Men
Herod
Adult Jesus
A small group of Jesus' followers.

SCRIPT

The family, except Sarah, are sitting around their dining table. It is Christmas Eve and examples of typical Christmas preparations are evident. The younger children are opening Christmas cards. Mum is wrapping presents and throughout gives the impression of being very busy in her preparations for Christmas. Sarah is at a separate table attending to her make-up.

Anna *(Sifting through the pile of cards)* It must be here somewhere. He never forgets to send us one.

Mum What are you looking for, Anna?

Anna The card from Uncle Z.

Tom *(Chanting, waving his hands in the air, and making gestures to indicate 'round the bend' and 'up the spire'. This is a family ritual, performed whenever Uncle Z is mentioned.)* 'Crazy Uncle Zechariah, round the bend and up the spire.'

Mum Stop that, Tom. I've told you before . . .

Tom Well, he is . . .

Sarah Weird.

Anna Well, I think he's nice. And he always sends us an unusual Christmas card.

Sarah Freaky!

Tom Not this year, sister.

Mum Anyway, he's away. Somewhere in the Far East. He's giving a lecture. Something clever about computers, I expect. You know what he's like.

Tom *(Laying a trap)* Who's that, Mum?

Mum	*(Falling for it)* Uncle Z . . .
Tom	*(Actions as before)* 'Crazy Uncle Zechariah, round the bend and up the spire.'
Mum	Stop that! Look, Tom, you get these presents wrapped up. I'm going to see if the turkey's thawed.
Tom	Why me? That's not fair. Anyway, I've got all these 'thank you' letters to write.
Anna	Tom, it's Christmas Eve. You haven't had any presents yet!
Tom	I know, but I like to write them in advance. Then you've got more time after Christmas to enjoy your prezzies. Anyway, why shouldn't *Sarah* do the wrapping-up?
Sarah	I wish you'd wrap up. Anyway, I've got to get ready for a party tonight.
Mum	Stop squabbling, you lot, and just get it done. *(Exit)*
Anna	Whose party, Sarah?
Sarah	Haven't decided yet. I've got six invitations to choose from. I'm still weighing up the talent.

(Tom takes out an envelope he's had hidden in his shirt and studies it.)

Anna	What've you got there, Tom?
Tom	*(Teasing)* I'm not sure. Looks like an envelope. Something quite heavy inside. Could be interesting. Very nice stamp. Let's see. Sing . . . a . . . pore . . .
Anna	You pig! That's the card from Uncle Z! Give it here!

(Anna tries to grab the card. Tom dances round the room, waving it, while she chases him.)

Tom	*(During the chase, with actions as before)* 'Crazy Uncle Zechariah, round the bend and up the spire.'
Mum	*(From offstage)* What's going on in there?
Tom	*(Sitting down innocently)* Nothing.

(Anna grabs the card and looks at it.)

Anna	I wonder what it will be this year.
Tom	What was last year's?
Anna	That was the one that changed colour every day for the twelve days of Christmas . . .
Sarah	Weird.
Tom	Yeah, and then self-destructed on January 6th. Pow!
Sarah	Freaky.
Tom	Well, go on then . . . open it.

(Anna gingerly opens the envelope. Sarah pretends not to be interested but is intrigued. From the envelope Anna takes a totally black rectangular piece of plastic. Tom and Anna are visibly puzzled, disappointed.)

Anna	It's . . . just black . . . all over.
Sarah	Great.
Tom	*(Picking up the envelope and removing a letter)* Wait a bit. There's a note here. *(Reading)* 'Hi there kids . . . hope you enjoy this. It's an XMAS CARD.'
Sarah	What a surprise!
Tom	No, listen. That's X.M.A.S.C.A.R.D.
Sarah	He can spell! The wonders of the National Curriculum!
Tom	Shut up, Sarah, and listen. *(Reading, but struggling)* It stands for something. It's an . . . **Ex**-is-tential, **M**ulti-di- . . . **m**ulti-dimensional, **a**na . . . *(Handing the letter to Sarah)* . . . what's that say?
Sarah	*(Reading, but also struggling)* It's an **Ex**istential, **M**ultidimensional, **A**na . . . ana . . . Anna, you read it. It's a bit fuzzy. I think I've got some mascara in my eyes.
Anna	*(Taking the letter and reading with ease)* It's an **Ex**istential, **M**ultidimensional, **A**nalogue **S**imulation with **C**hromoscopic, **A**utomated **R**eal-time **D**isplay.
Tom	I knew that's what it was.
Anna	*(Reading on)* 'Turn towards the light. Hold the card steady in front of you. Focus on your own reflection. Concentrate hard. And you may find out what Christmas is really all about.' Shall we try it?
Sarah	*(Snatching it and trying)* Let's have a look then. *(Dismissive)* Can't see a thing. *(Handing it back to Anna)* Anyway, I know what Christmas is all about.

Tom	Oh, yeah?
Sarah	*(Resuming her make-up)* Yeah. *(Cynically)* Parties. And prezzies.
Anna	*(Looking into the card, gradually getting excited)* Look, Tom, I think I can see something.
Tom	Let's see.

(He joins Anna and they study the card.)

Anna	It looks like . . . lots of houses . . . and streets . . . and . . .
Tom	Oh, yes. It's a bit dark, but, yes, look, can you see, crowds of people . . .

(Lights go down on the family as the lights begin to come up on the area set aside for the events of the first Christmas.)

Anna	See that man and the young woman, coming down the street? Do you think it's . . . ?
Tom	Of course . . . it's Bethlehem!

Song 1: Silently down to this world

The first Christmas area is dimly lit, suggesting night-time. A crowd of citizens stands motionless, facing to one side, spread randomly around the area available. This song is sung by the crowd, supplemented by the choir. If an adult choir is involved the song would be most effective sung in four-part harmony.

Towards the end of the first verse, Mary and Joseph enter. They weave their way slowly through the crowd, who ignore them.

1. Silently down to this world, his creation,
   from heaven's glory comes Jesus the Lord.
   No trumpet fanfare, no loud acclamation,
   herald the coming of Jesus the Lord.

   *Suddenly and silently, Emmanuel is here,
   quietly, surprisingly, the way of God is clear.
   Gently to this world below to take away all fear,
   softly, the Prince of Peace, Jesus draws near.
   Ah . . .*

(During the second verse, one person, representing the innkeeper, directs Mary and Joseph to the stable, off-stage. They leave during the chorus.)

2. Stand now in awe of this great revelation:
   God is made human in Jesus the Lord.
   No pomp, no clamour, no great demonstration,
   humbly from glory comes Jesus the Lord.

   Chorus

3. Humbly approach him in hushed expectation,
   hearts full of wonder at Jesus the Lord.
   Nothing to offer, no great demonstration,
   in quiet faith know the peace of the Lord.

   Chorus

(The crowd stay motionless and the lights go down. The lights come up again on the family.)

Tom	Wow! That's magic! It's like a Christmas card with three-dimensional moving pictures.
Anna	It's almost like, real. As if you were actually there.
Tom	Come and look, Sarah.
Sarah	Not now, thank you, children. Much too busy. I've got to scrape this make-up off and start again. And someone's going to have to wrap all those presents or we'll be scraping Mum off the ceiling. And I still haven't decided which invitation to accept.
Anna	Why was everyone ignoring them, Tom?
Tom	Sorry?
Anna	In the card. Joseph and Mary. I mean, no-one seemed to take much notice of them.
Mum	*(Entering, looking frantic)* Panic stations! The turkey's still frozen. Where's the hair-dryer? *(Looking around and calling out instructions as she hunts)* Haven't you wrapped those presents yet? Sarah, don't forget to ring Granny. Tom, do something about all the tinsel

	that's fallen off the tree. Anna, when you're ready we need the table setting for tomorrow's lunch. And have you seen my list?
Tom	*(Picking up a bit of paper)* Is this it, Mum? Countdown to Christmas.
Mum	That's it. What's the next thing on the list?
Tom	Nervous breakdown.
Anna	Mum, why did everyone in Bethlehem ignore Mary and Joseph?
Mum	I expect they were very busy.
Tom	Sounds familiar.
Anna	But why wasn't there room for them? Why did they have to go and stay in a stable?
Mum	Well, the town was very crowded.
Tom	Why was it so busy, Mum?
Mum	I think there was a census thing going on and everyone had to go back to their family's town.
Tom	What's a senseless thing, Mum?
Sarah	You are, twit.
Mum	Look, I haven't time for all these questions now. We'll never be ready at this rate. *(Exit)*
Tom	Perhaps if we look in the card, Anna . . .

(They return to study the card. The lighting again changes.)

Song 2: Busy at Christmas

The crowd come to life and move around busily greeting one another and so on. A group of census officers enter. They are carrying clip boards and pencils. As the opening chords for Song 2 begin, the crowd quietens down and the census officers take centre stage.

INTRODUCTION (sung as a kind of proclamation).

1. **Census officers** — Augustus Caesar has decreed
a census here in Bethlehem.
We're counting all the people and
recording every one of them.
We're sorting them according to
their individual fam'ly trees,
And putting men and women, boys
and girls in diff'rent . . . categ'ries.

In the three verses that follow the crowd give details of their identities, pointing to various individuals, while the census officers frantically try to record these. Then they try to recount what they have written, without much success, finally giving up in despair.

Crowd plus Choir — There's Jacob and Hannah, their daughters, Joanna,
Rebekah and Martha, Abijah, their son.
There's cousin Zipporah and Auntie Deborah,
with Ezra their father, from Bethany come.

2. **Census officers** — *(Checking off various members of the crowd)*
One, two, three, four, five, six, seven, eight.
That's Jacob and Hannah and Martha, Joanna,
Rebekah et cet'ra, a fam'ly of ten.
Oh, now we're befuddled and horribly muddled,
perhaps we had better start over again.

Crowd plus Choir — There's Matthew and Leah, from north of Gibeah,
and old Obadiah. We almost forgot,
there's Ruth and Nathanael, Rachel and Daniel,
young Hezekiah, the Jericho lot.

3. **Census officers** — *(As before)*
One, two, three, four, five, six, seven, eight.
That's Ruth and Nathanael, Rachel and Daniel,
a woman called Leah, a couple of men.
It's all quite bemusing and really confusing,
perhaps we had better start over again.

Crowd plus Choir — There's Naomi's mother and Benjamin's brother,
with Sarah their nanny and Esther their niece.

Her uncle's the geezer who's called Ebenezer,
his auntie's the granny of Eli the priest.

4. Census officers *(As before)*
One, two, three, four, five, six, seven, eight.
That's somebody's mother and someone or other,
a nanny, a granny, and someone called Ben.
This town is so busy, we're getting quite dizzy,
we'll just have to leave it and come back again.

(Census officers leave in despair)

Crowd The town's so very busy with the census,
the inns are full, no room for anyone.
There isn't time to stop and notice Jesus,
there's just too much that must be done.
We're rushing round to visit one another,
it's all so busy here in Bethlehem.
We've heard about the baby and his mother,
but haven't time to give to them.

Crowd and choir sing alternate lines in canon. The overall effect should sound very busy and frantic:

Crowd The town's so very busy with the census,
Choir *The town's so very busy with the census,*
Crowd the inns are full, no room for anyone.
Choir *The inns are full, no room for anyone.*
Crowd there isn't time to stop and notice Jesus,
Choir *There isn't time to stop and notice Jesus,*
Crowd there's just too much that must be done.
Choir *there's just too much that must be done.*
Crowd We're rushing round to visit one another,
Choir *They're rushing round to visit one another,*
Crowd it's all so busy here in Bethlehem.
Choir *it's all so busy there in Bethlehem.*
Crowd We've heard about the baby and his mother,
Choir *They've heard about the baby and his mother,*
Crowd but haven't time to give to them.
Choir *but haven't time to give to them.*

(The lights come up on the family as the above verse ends. Mum has rejoined the children. Tom's line is over the four bars of link music. Then the family sing.)

Tom That's what I meant. It's just as bad today, isn't it!

5. Family The world is busy celebrating Christmas,
the usual rush and panic have begun.
There isn't time to stop and think of Jesus,
there's just too much that must be done.
They're rushing round from one thing to another,
the streets and shops are crowded once again.
They've heard about the baby and his mother,
but haven't time to give to them.

Crowd plus half the choir sing one line, while the family plus the other half of the choir sing alternate lines in canon. Again, it should all sound very busy and frantic:

Crowd plus Choir A The town's so very busy with the census,
Family plus Choir B *The world is busy celebrating Christmas,*
Crowd plus Choir A the inns are full, no room for anyone.
Family plus Choir B *the usual rush and panic have begun.*
Crowd plus Choir A There isn't time to stop and think of Jesus,
Family plus Choir B *there's just too much that must be done.*

Crowd plus Choir A	there's just too much that must be done.	
Family plus Choir B	*They're rushing round to visit one another,*	
Crowd plus Choir A	They're rushing round from one thing to another,	
Family plus Choir B	*it's all so busy here in Bethlehem.*	
Crowd plus Choir A	the streets and shops are crowded once again.	
Family plus Choir B	*They've heard about the baby and his mother,*	
Crowd plus Choir A	They've heard about the baby and his mother,	
Family plus Choir B	*but haven't time to give to them.*	
Crowd plus Choir A	but haven't time to give to them.	

———

(All the crowd leave the central area and Mum leaves the room during the last line of the song. The lighting for the first Christmas area goes down.)

Anna	Well, I'm not going to be too busy at Christmas to think of Jesus.
Tom	Nor am I. Perhaps I'll leave these 'thank you' letters for Boxing Day.
Sarah	Steady on.
Anna	Let's see what else is in the card.
Tom	Right.

(They study the card again.)

Anna	I want to see the baby and his mother.
Tom	Yes, in the stable, with the baby Jesus lying in the manger.
Anna	Just like a proper Christmas card.
Tom	Look, it's coming. Can you see?
Anna	Yes, that's it. Look, Sarah, come and see.
Sarah	Oh, alright. *(Coming across to look)* I'll never be ready at this rate. *(She takes the card and studies it in an unconvinced fashion.)*
Anna	Can you see it?
Sarah	Oh, yes.
Tom	What can you see, Sarah?
Sarah	It looks like . . . a totally plain piece of black plastic. It's rubbish. *(She throws it down on the table dismissively and returns to her make-up.)*
Anna	Careful! You'll break it. *(She picks the card up and she and Tom return to studying it.)*
Tom	And it's not rubbish. If you concentrate, you can see what Christmas is really all about. It's just like Uncle Z said.
Sarah	*(Doing the chant and actions)* 'Crazy Uncle Zechariah, round the bend and up the spire.'

(Tom and Anna ignore her.)

Tom	Mary looks very thoughtful, doesn't she, Anna. I wonder what she's thinking?
Anna	Probably wondering why her baby is so special.

(The opening bars of Song 3 begin as the lights on the modern-day family go down.)

Tom	Funny, 'cos I was wondering that as well.

3. Here in the manger

Mary is sitting beside the manger, watching over the baby Jesus.

Verse 1 and the first chorus should, if possible, be a solo sung by Mary. The choir joins in from Verse 2. There is a descant to be added in the final chorus.

1. **Mary** Here in the manger, light is descending
   into our darkness; we welcome the dawn
   shining from heaven – the night is now ending –
   light in a stable is born.

   *Come now, my soul, magnify God above;
   rejoice, my spirit, and tell of his love!
   Glory to God, sing his praises*

9

> *for sending Jesus, his son.*

2. **Choir** Here in the manger, new hope is springing,
    hope for a world which seemed lost and forlorn.
    God's promised gift of salvation now bringing,
    hope in a stable is born.

    Chorus

3. Here in the manger, peacefully sleeping,
    enters a world with hostility torn,
    God's prince of peace, now his promises keeping:
    peace in a stable is born.

    Chorus

4. Here in the manger, God's love is lying,
    clothed with his grace, our humanity worn;
    for our salvation, his glory denying:
    love in a stable is born.

    Chorus, with descant

(The lighting changes again from the first Christmas to the family. The two younger children are still studying the card.)

Anna What can you see now, Tom?

Tom It's all very dark still. Wait a bit, though. I think I can see some stars.

Anna And look, there's some men coming down that hill.

Tom Got it. Scruffy looking bunch, aren't they?

Anna What's that funny smell?

Tom *(Sniffing and making an appropriate disgusted noise)* I don't know. It smells like . . . sheep dung.

(Lights change.)

Song 4: The shepherds' shuffle

The central area is empty. The shepherds shuffle on, looking round, bemused. The opening chord sounds and they launch into the song. The point and humour of this song is that it would take something spectacular to get these hardened shepherds excited. And something spectacular has happened! Even so, when they do respond by dancing the shepherds' shuffle it is still very restrained. There is opportunity here for some inventive choreography for the shepherds' dance in each chorus. The song should be sung entirely by the group of shepherds, but they could be supported by the choir, if necessary.

1. **Shepherds** Now we are humble shepherds, from the hills up there we come;
    we do not get much to shout about, our lives are quite hum-drum.
    It would take a lot our imperturbability to ruffle,
    but tonight we're so excited we could do the shepherds' shuffle!

(with dance) *Singing oy-yoy-yoy-yoy-yoy-yoy, oom-pah-pah,
shuffle slowly to the left, but not too far.
Not too quickly, quite sedately, turn around, with
both our footsies firmly on the ground.
Moving with the steady pace we shepherds keep –
after all, we wouldn't want to scare the sheep –
then we raise our crooks and point them to the sky, and
take a little break to worship God . . . on high.*

(Shepherds assemble along the front of the stage)

Shepherd A I was gath'ring in the flocks,

Shepherd B and I was counting sheep.

Shepherd C I was washing dirty socks,

Shepherd D and I was trying to sleep.

Shepherd E I was cooking shepherd's pie,

All it was the dead of night,
when these angels filled the sky

	and made the darkness turn . . . to light!
2.	A thousand angels, shining bright, announced the Saviour's birth, singing, 'Glory be to God on high and peace to us on earth.' So, then, how could we respond to such a wonderful kerfuffle? Well, now, obviously, it had to be, to do the shepherds' shuffle!
	Chorus (as before)

(Shepherds assemble along the front of the stage)

Shepherd C	I just left my socks to dry,
Shepherd B	there wasn't time to pack.
Shepherd E	Gave the sheep the shepherd's pie
Shepherd A	and told them we'd be back.
Shepherd D	God has spoken, we must act,
All	although it's dead of night, if the angel's word is fact our darkness soon will turn . . . to light!
3.	The angel said we'd find him in a stable hereabout, so we've now arrived in Bethlehem to check the story out. If we find the baby nothing then our songs of joy will muffle, given half the chance, we'll even dance and do the shepherds' shuffle!
	Chorus (as before) – repeat first line as many times as necessary, until all shepherds are off-stage.

(Shepherds shuffle off. Lighting stays up. Wise Men enter at the back of the hall, ready for their cue. They are, of course, carrying the necessary gifts. Tom and Anna are still studying the card.)

Tom	Look, there are some more people heading for Bethlehem!
Anna	Of course, it's . . .
Tom & Anna	. . . the three wise men!

Song 5: March of the wise men

The three wise men sing their first verse from the back of the hall.

1. **Wise men**	Here we come, the famous three wise men, we are on our way to Bethlehem. Gold and frankincense and myrrh we bring, as an off'ring for the new-born King!

The wise men march forward, acting appropriately, while the choir sings their verse:

Choir	Here they come, the famous three wise men, they are on their way to Bethlehem. Gold and frankincense and myrrh they bring, as an off'ring for the new-born king!

From the front of the hall the wise men sing their second verse pointing to the star and to Bethlehem, offstage somewhere.

2. **Wise men**	He's the one the star is pointing to, he's the ancient promise now come true. We are confident of this one thing: that this baby is the new-born king!

During the choir's second verse the Wise Men proceed to the central area of the stage.

Choir	He's the one the star is pointing to, he's the ancient promise now come true. We are confident of this one thing: that this baby is the new-born king!

During the final verse, the wise men consult maps, check the star's position, point to Bethlehem, and so on, then exit, as the verse finishes.

3. **Choir (in 2 parts)**	Here they come, the famous three wise men, they are on their way to Bethlehem. Gold and frankincense and myrrh they bring,

> as an off'ring for the new-born king!
> He's the one the star is pointing to,
> he's the ancient promise now come true.
> We are confident of this one thing:
> that this baby is the new-born king!

(Lighting changes from the first Christmas to the family.)

Anna Oh, Sarah, if only you could see it! *(All in a rush)* There's the shepherds and they've seen this angel and he tells them that a special baby's been born and he'll be the saviour of the world and they're going to Bethlehem to find him and he's born in a stable because the inns are full and they're looking for him and there's the wise men and they've come from the east and they've seen this star and they're following it and they're going to Bethlehem too and they're all going to worship the baby, and they're taking these gifts, and there's gold and there's myrrh and there's . . . um . . . um . . .

Tom . . . frankenstein.

Sarah Frankincense, idiot. Besides, I hate babies.

Tom What is it, anyway, that franken-whatsit? And myrrh, what's that?

(Mum comes back into the room, still in a panic.)

Mum I'll never get that turkey thawed out in time. I still can't find the hair dryer.

Sarah Try the microwave.

Tom The hair dryer in the microwave?

Sarah No, I meant put the turkey in the microwave, to defrost it.

Tom Have you seen the size of the turkey? It's like an ostrich.

Anna Mum, can you stop for a minute?

Mum *(Sitting down)* Alright, one minute.

Anna You know the wise men who went to Bethlehem to see Jesus.

Mum Yes.

Anna And they took gold and myrrh and that other stuff.

Mum Yes.

Anna Well, what was it all about? I mean, why didn't they take him a rattle . . .

Tom . . . or a blanket, or something like that, something for a baby. Anyway what is that myrrh stuff and that franken-thingy?

Mum I suppose they were sort of symbols.

Tom Cymbals? What, like in the orchestra? Crash, bang, wallop!

Mum No, symbols. Things that mean something. Like gold is a gift for a king.

(Sarah begins to listen with half an ear.)

Anna So, was Jesus a king?

Mum In a way. But he didn't rule a country, like an ordinary king.

Tom And what about the other stuff, were they timbrels as well?

Sarah Symbols, pea-brain. Why don't you listen!

Mum Yes, I think so. Frankincense was some kind of special stuff which people used to burn when they prayed. When this lovely smelling smoke rose up into the air people thought it was a special offering to God.

Anna And what about myrrh?

Mum Um. That's the sad present.

Tom How do you mean, sad? Like, the presents I always get from Aunty Edna?

Mum No. Not that. It's just that myrrh was a special perfume that they used for putting on people's bodies when they died.

Tom Ugh! Why give that to a baby?

Mum Well, perhaps they had some idea of what would happen when he grew up, that Jesus would have to suffer and . . . oh, never mind, we don't want to spoil Christmas by thinking about that. Now I must get on! *(She starts to leave the room.)*

Tom	*(As Mum leaves the room)* Countdown to Christmas . . . five, four, three, two, one, panic!
Anna	What did Mum mean? About what would happen when the baby grew up?
Sarah	Why don't you look in your clever card and find out, eh?
Tom	Why don't you?!
Sarah	Alright. Maybe I will.

(Sarah now takes the card, away from the other two children, and stands studying it. The lighting changes again.)

Song 6: High on a hillside

This song, sung by the choir, uses the same music as 'Here in a manger' (Song 3). This is to underline the notion that it was the same Jesus in the manger who became the man Jesus, who preached the kingdom of heaven, who was proclaimed to be the son of God, who gave his life on the cross for our sins and who rose again and ascended to heaven. During this song, four incidents from the life of the adult Jesus are mimed on stage. To begin with, the central stage area is completely clear.

1. The sermon on the mount

The adult Jesus enters followed by a small group of people. He takes a position in one corner and stands as though preaching. The group of followers sit at his feet. During the chorus, Jesus moves to another corner.

> High on a hillside Jesus is preaching,
> crowds gather round him, attending his word.
> Those who are wise will respond to his teaching:
> 'Seek first the kingdom of God.'
>
> *Thank you, Lord Jesus, for climbing that hill,*
> *thank you, Lord Jesus, for doing God's will.*
> *Glory to God, sing his praises*
> *for sending Jesus, his Son.*

2. The Transfiguration

During this verse Jesus kneels to pray, looks up and raises his arms towards heaven. Three of the followers approach cautiously, but stop suddenly as though stunned by the brightness of the light and the voice from heaven. During the chorus, Jesus moves to another corner.

> High on a hillside Jesus is praying,
> round him his glory shines bright as the day.
> Then from the heavens we hear someone saying:
> 'This is my Son, him obey.'
>
> *Chorus*

3. The Crucifixion

Jesus stands with his back to the audience and raises his arms as though being crucified. Some of the followers crouch nearby with threatening postures, representing those who cried 'crucify him', while others kneel with their heads buried in their hands with grief. During the chorus, Jesus moves to a fourth corner.

> High on a hillside Jesus is dying,
> sinless one, suff'ring for wrongs we have done.
> 'Now it is finished,' triumphantly crying!
> Vict'ry o'er death he has won.
>
> *Chorus*

4. The Ascension

Jesus raises his arms towards heaven, looks back at the group of followers and leaves. They raise their hands and close their eyes to represent their receiving the Holy Spirit. During the chorus they leave the stage.

> High on a hillside, Jesus ascending,
> risen Lord bidding farewell to his friends.
> Then from his glory his spirit he's sending,
> until he comes back again.
>
> *Chorus*

(Lighting changes again. Sarah is standing, looking at the card, visibly moved. The other children are looking in her direction.)

Anna	Well?
Tom	Did you see anything?
Sarah	Might have done.
Tom	She did see something. You see, Sarah, we told you.
Anna	What was it?
Sarah	Nothing. It was nothing. *(Throwing the card back on the table.)* Just a bit of black plastic. That's all it is. *(She starts to leave the room.)* But you do know they killed him in the end, don't you?
Tom	Who?

(Sarah leaves the room.)

Anna	I think she means . . . Jesus.

(Mum enters the room and overhears the conversation.)

Tom	What? Someone killed the baby Jesus?
Mum	No, but Herod tried.
Tom	Why?
Mum	Well, when the wise men got to Jerusalem, on their way to Bethlehem they went to King Herod's palace, because they thought that that was where they'd find a new king.
Tom	I bet Herod didn't like that!
Mum	No, he didn't like the idea of a new king at all. So he gave orders to kill all the baby boys in the area. He must've been a really nasty character.
Anna	What? Surely no-one would try to harm a little baby.
Mum	I'm afraid you'll have to learn that wherever there is good there is also evil. Herod was just the start of a battle between good and evil which went on all through Jesus's life, until . . . in the end . . . look, I must get on. And you'd better get this lot tidied up or there'll be a battle going on here soon! *(Exit)*
Tom	I don't get this bit about Herod.
Anna	Let's have another look in the card and see what's going on.

(Lighting changes again.)

Song 7: Herod the terror

The central area is clear.

INTRODUCTION

Choir Ev'ryone look out! Trouble is about!
When Herod curses and blasphemes,
let all beware his evil schemes. Look out!

Herod enters, announcing himself with an evil laugh. A group of young children rush, screaming in terror, around the hall, hiding themselves under seats and so on. It could be effective for the part of Herod to be taken by an adult with a bass voice.

1. Herod I'm Herod, the terror, and all the powers of darkness
are focusing on Bethlehem tonight.
I'm jealous of Jesus, I'm ruthless and I'm heartless,
I'll do my worst to terminate the light.

The Wise Men enter and confer with Herod during the Choir's verse. Herod sends them away, then looks furious, shakes fist, walks around stamping his feet, etc.

Choir He's Herod, the terror, and all the powers of darkness
are focusing on Bethlehem tonight.
He's jealous of Jesus, he's ruthless and he's heartless,
he'll do his worst to terminate the light.
The light of the world is Jesus,

perfectly holy and true,
righteousness shines from his presence,
with power to make all things new.
But evil opposes goodness,
for wrong cannot stand with right.
Hatred strives with the love of God,
and darkness scorns the light.
Look out!

Herod repeats the evil laugh. The group of young children run screaming around the hall briefly and hide again.

2. Herod I'm Herod, the terror, I'm causing utter mayhem,
distress and pain my cruel plan will bring.
My forces are searching for infant boys to slay them,
determined to destroy this new-born king.

A group of soldiers enter and confer with Herod during the Choir's verse, then exit as though setting off to hunt down children.

Choir He's Herod, the terror, he's causing utter mayhem,
distress and pain his cruel plan will bring.
His forces are searching for infant boys to slay them,
determined to destroy the new-born king.

The young children all run off with the soldiers in pursuit in the link between musical sections here. Herod continues to act as though furious and threatened.

The king of all kings is Jesus,
noble and worthy is he.
He is the truth sent from heaven,
with power and authority.
Now falsehood and cruel injustice
with justice and truth contend.
But the power of the love of God
must triumph in the end.
Must triumph in the end.
Must triumph in the end.

Herod exits in anger, during the closing dramatic discords of the song, emitting one final scream of despair as the song finishes.

(The lighting changes back to focusing on the family. Anna and Tom are distressed. Sarah enters as they start talking and overhears their conversation.)

Tom Fancy that Herod trying to kill Jesus!

Anna It's horrible!

Tom And all those baby boys being murdered.

Anna I didn't like that bit. That's not what I expect to see in a Christmas card.

Sarah *(Quite aggressively)* Oh no. You don't like to think about that side of the story, do you? That there were people that wanted to dispose of Jesus. You forget about the fact that Jesus had to grow up, that he had to battle against evil all his life, that he had to suffer, and that in the end they arrested him for nothing at all and had him put to death on a cross. Oh no. You'd like to keep him as a cute little baby lying in a manger full of straw, a sweet little Christmas card scene, in a nice clean stable with all the animals standing around with drippy expressions on their faces. Typical.

(She picks up her make-up and walks out. The other two are stunned by this outburst momentarily. Then, suddenly, simultaneously they look at each other and get the same idea . . .)

Tom & Anna The animals!

Tom We haven't seen them yet!

Anna *(Picking up the card and looking into it)* There ought to be some animals in a stable.

Tom *(Also looking)* Come on, where are you? Just the odd camel . . .

Anna . . . or a donkey . . .

(The lighting changes again.)

Tom & Anna A donkey!

Song 8: All of God's creatures can celebrate

The baby in the manger, Mary and Joseph are all in place now in the area representing the first Christmas, as in the traditional nativity scene.

This song is intended to be a little light relief, to contrast with the serious content of the previous two songs. It would lend itself to audience participation in the chorus from Verse 2 onwards. The four animals enter in turn during the introductory music for their verse. They should be in appropriate animal costumes, or at least wearing animal masks.

The donkey enters...

1. Donkey Now I may be an ass with a face like a clown,
I may be the stubbornest creature in town,
and I'll have to concede that my brain is not great,
but even a donkey can celebrate!

Choir Even a donkey can celebrate!

During the chorus the donkey and Joseph join in some appropriate jiving.

Chorus **Choir** *Celebrate! celebrate, the party's begun!*
All of God's creatures can join in the fun!
So whoever you are, step right in through the door,
he welcomes the rich and he welcomes the poor,
the high and the mighty, the lowly in state:
all of God's creatures can celebrate!
All of God's creatures can celebrate!

The hen enters...

2. Hen Now I'm only a hen and I live in this shed,
and that little child is asleep in my bed!
I may only produce the boiled egg on your plate,
but even a chicken can celebrate!

Choir Even a chicken can celebrate!

The hen, donkey and Joseph dance together...

Choir *Celebrate! celebrate ... etc*

The camel enters...

3. Camel Now I am an old camel and I know my place.
If you think you're ugly take a look at my face.
I am simply a beast designed to carry a weight,
but even a camel can celebrate!

Choir Even a camel can celebrate!

The camel, hen, donkey and Joseph dance together...

Choir *Celebrate! celebrate ... etc*

The cow enters...

4. Cow I am only a beast with a diet of grass,
I'm not very bright and I'm real working class,
I've been stuck in the cowshed, and that's why I'm late :

(Music stops)

(Spoken) ... I had udder business to attend to ...

(Music restarts)

But even the cattle can celebrate!

Choir Even the cattle can celebrate!

The cow, camel, hen, donkey and Joseph dance together...

Choir *Celebrate! celebrate ... etc. (Repeat last line.)*

(The animals take up positions around the manger and Joseph returns to his position. This is the beginning of a typical nativity scene tableau. The lighting on the tableau stays on now as the lighting on the family comes up. Anna and Tom are still looking into the card.)

Anna Look, it's beginning to look like a proper Christmas card scene now. With the baby in the manger and Joseph and Mary and the animals.

Tom	Yeah. And it's about time the shepherds turned up at the stable.
Anna	And the wise men. I'd like to see them come to the stable as well.
Tom	Keep concentrating like he said.
Anna	I wish . . .
Tom	What?
Anna	I don't know. I just wish that somehow – well, look, see our reflections in the card.
Tom	Yes. Clearly as anything. There we are.
Anna	Well, I wish that we could really be in there as well. You know, somehow, go to the stable ourselves and worship Jesus.
Tom	Concentrate, he said, and you'll find out what Christmas is really all about . . .
Anna	I'm concentrating . . .

Song 9: Come to the stable

During this song the tableau on stage is gradually built up until a complete Christmas card nativity scene is assembled, with shepherds, wise men, other citizens from Bethlehem, the two younger children, and finally, responding to the adult Jesus, Sarah. The song is sung by the choir, apart from the first half of Verse 5 which should be a solo.

1. Now in your heart, you can come
    to Bethlehem, to the stable, to worship God the son.
    Come now to him, just believe,
    in faith draw near, his love receive.
    From heaven's glory he laid aside his royal crown,
    humbled himself and for our salvation stepped right down.
    So you can come to the stable, a place is for you set apart:
    but will he find a place within your heart?

During the second verse the shepherds enter and take their places, kneeling in in worship around the manger.

2. Down from the hills, shepherds, come
    to Bethlehem, to the stable, to worship God the son.
    Come now to him, just believe,
    in faith draw near, his love receive.
    You heard the angels announce the promised saviour's birth,
    singing of glory to God and peace for those on earth.
    So, shepherds, come to the stable, a place is for you set apart:
    but will he find a place within your heart?

During the third verse the wise men enter, offer their gifts, and take their places, kneeling in worship around the manger.

3. Far from the East, wise men come
    to Bethlehem, to the stable, to worship God the son.
    Come now to him, just believe,
    in faith draw near, his love receive.
    Follow the star which revealed the chosen time and place,
    where God's anointed descends to save the human race.
    So, wise men, come to the stable, a place is for you set apart:
    but will he find a place within your heart?

During the fourth verse a number of citizens of Bethlehem enter one or two at a time and join the tableau.

4. All in this world, you can come
    to Bethlehem, to the stable, to worship God the son.
    Come now to him, just believe,
    in faith draw near, his love receive.
    He left the riches of heaven our poverty to share,
    entered our world to establish heaven's kingdom here.
    So you can come to the stable, a place is for you set apart:
    but will he find a place within your heart?

During the repeat of Verse 1 which follows, Tom and Anna place the card, standing up, on the table and slowly walk backwards, until eventually they find themselves, to their surprise, entering the tableau. They look bewildered, amazed, delighted, and then kneel in worship themselves.

Repeat Verse 1

During the link into Verse 5, Sarah enters the room, picks up the card and starts to study it. As the verse starts the adult Jesus enters and stands behind her, with his arms raised in invitation. Sarah clearly responds to the words of the song and the invitation, although she does not look directly at the adult Jesus. She is seeing him in the card, of course.

5. Solo Open your eyes, look up high,
there on a cross see the one son of God who was born to die.
Look up to him, just believe,
in faith draw near, new life receive.

Choir Open your eyes now and see the love of God for you,
look up to Jesus the saviour, dying there for you.
He offers life by his death, it's for you that he suffers and dies.
Look now to him, believe, and open your eyes!

Adult Jesus *(Spoken over link music to Verse 6)*
One more invitation, Sarah.
I came to live and to die for you.
Come to me. *(Exit slowly)*

As this final verse begins Sarah puts the card down on the table; she then follows the same procedure as the other two children to take her place in worship in the tableau.

6. Now in your heart, you can come
to Bethlehem, to the stable, to worship God the son.
Come now to him, just believe,
in faith draw near, his love receive.
He left the riches of heaven our poverty to share,
entered our world to establish heaven's kingdom here.
So you can come to the stable, a place is for you set apart.
Will Jesus find a place within your heart?

(Towards the end of the song an old man with a long beard, a caricature of a professor type enters and stands thoughtfully to one side observing the scene. It is, of course, Uncle Z. After a while, Anna looks up and sees him. She reacts appropriately.)

Anna Look, it's . . .

Anna, Tom and Sarah Uncle Z!

(They gather and converse at the front of stage.)

Tom How did you get here?

Uncle Z Easy, really, just a matter of modulating the parallel transdimensional interface vectors, with a quasi-algorithmic non-Euclidean matrix, and then . . . look, never mind, aren't you pleased to see me?

Sarah Of course, we are, but . . . what are you doing here?

Uncle Z Well, I thought that the invitation was for everyone. *(Doing the actions)* Even 'Crazy Uncle Zechariah, round the bend and up the spire.'

Tom How did you . . . ?

Uncle Z Never mind. Did you enjoy the Christmas card?

Anna It was the best Christmas card ever. We saw all about the shepherds coming to the stable, and the wise men with their gifts.

Tom And nasty Herod trying to kill the baby.

Sarah And it made us remember that Jesus wasn't just a baby. He was God's Son and came to bring us into his kingdom by dying for us on the cross.

Tom And that, even people today can come to the stable and worship him. In their hearts.

Uncle Z Now that is what Christmas is really all about! And that's something worth having a party for. Come on, let's celebrate!

Anna, Tom and Sarah Hooray!

Uncle Z Ring the bells! Sound the trumpets! Beat the drums!

Sarah	Sorry, Uncle Z, but we haven't got a bell.
Tom	We haven't got a trumpet!
Anna	We haven't got a drum!
Uncle Z	Who cares! We can pretend, can't we!

Song 10: If we had a bell

Everyone on stage comes to life and joins in with the choir to sing the final song. There is opportunity for some four-part singing in this song.

All   If we had a bell, we'd bang it, clang it, bong it, dong it, ring-a-ding-ding it.
But we haven't so we'll sing it!

Men   Bing! Bong! Bing! Bong! Bing! Bong! Bing! Bong!

All   Ding, dong, ding, dong, ding, dong, ding, dong,
let all the bells ring out this song:
now Jesus Christ is born our king,
ding, dong, ding, dong, ding-a-dong-a-ding.

If we had a drum, we'd bash it, crash it, tap it, rap it, bang it, beat it.
But we haven't so we'll bleat it!
Bom, bom, bom, bom, bom, bom, bom,
borra bom, bom, bom, bom, bom,
bom, bom, bom, bom, bom, bom, bom, borra-borra bom.

If we had a harp, we'd twang it, clang it, pluck it, strum it, finger and thumb it.
But we haven't so we'll hum it!

(Hum 'Angels from the realms of glory')

If we had a horn, trombone or trumpet,
we'd raise it, sound it, play all around it,
pump it, prime it, tune it, chime it.
But we haven't so we'll mime it!

(Mime playing brass instruments: add sound effects if desired, to tune of 'Good King Wenceslas'.)

If we had a card, we'd read it, write it, lick it, bend it, stick it, send it.
But we haven't, so pretend it:
we wish you a merry Christmas,
we wish you a merry Christmas,
we wish you a merry Christmas and a happy new . . .

If we were angels up in heaven, we would praise him, sing hallelujah.
But we're not, we're here, but we'll still sing it to yer! (groan!)
Hallelujah! Hallelujah! Hallelujah! Hallelujah!

Now we haven't got a bell to bang it, clang it, bong it, dong it, ring-a-ding-a-ding it,
haven't got a drum to bash it, crash it, tap it, rap it, bang it, beat it,
haven't got a harp to twang it, clang it, pluck it, strum it, finger and thumb it,
haven't got a horn, trombone or trumpet, to raise it, sound it, play all around it, pump it, prime it, tune it, chime it,
haven't got a card to read it, write it, lick it, bend it, stick it, send it,
so we'll join with angels up in heaven, sing his praises, shout hallelujah!

Glory now to God we sing,
give thanks for Jesus born our king,
rejoice in praise before him.
O come let us adore him, Christ the Lord!

(At the conclusion of the song, everyone on stage takes a bow. As any applause dies down, Mum enters the area set aside for the modern-day family.)

Mum   Panic over, everyone. The hair dryer was in the bread bin. And I've decided to forget about the turkey. We're having sausages . . . oh, where are they all?
(Looks around) Tut! Just look at the mess they've left this place in.
(Starts to tidy up -- picks up the card) What on earth is this? No idea. Never mind, better get on. *(Laughing to herself, as she opens a drawer in the table)* Huh, countdown to Christmas, five, four, three, two, one . . .

(She puts the card in the drawer and slams it shut. Simultaneously there is blackout.)

Version 2

In this version of the musical, the action on the stage which depicts the story of the first Christmas, is linked by a series of Bible readings, rather than by the story of the modern-day family used in Version 1. It is intended that most of the acting be done by young people, in costume. The choir could be an adult choir, or a young people's choir, or a combination of the two, as in Version 1.

CAST

Mary and Joseph
Crowd of Citizens in Bethlehem
Group of Census Officers
Group of Shepherds (at least five)
Three Wise Men
Herod
Readers 1 and 2

BIBLE READINGS

Reader 1 But you, O Bethlehem, though you are small among the clans of Judah, out of you will come for me one who will be ruler over Israel, whose origins are from of old, from ancient times. (Micah 5.2)

Reader 2 This is the oracle of one who hears the words of God, who has knowledge from the Most High: I see him, but not now; I behold him, but not near. A star will come out of Jacob; a sceptre will rise out of Israel. (Numbers 24.16-17)

Reader 1 This is how the birth of Jesus Christ came about:

Reader 2 His mother Mary was pledged to be married to Joseph, but before they came together, she was found to be with child through the Holy Spirit. Because Joseph was a righteous man and did not want to expose her to public disgrace, he had in mind to divorce her quietly. But after he had considered this, an angel of the Lord appeared to him in a dream and said,

Reader 1 'Joseph son of David, do not be afraid to take Mary home as your wife, because what is conceived in her is from the Holy Spirit. She will give birth to a son, and you are to give him the name Jesus, because he will save his people from their sins.'

Reader 2 All this took place to fulfil what the Lord had said through the prophet:

Reader 1 'The virgin will be with child and will give birth to a son, and they will call him Emmanuel'

Reader 2 Which means, 'God with us.' (Matthew 1.18-23)

Song 1: Silently down to this world

Action on stage as in Version 1 (see page 6).

Reader 1 In those days Caesar Augustus issued a decree that a census should be taken of the entire Roman world. And everyone went to their own town to register.

Reader 2 So Joseph went up from the town of Nazareth in Galilee to Judea, to Bethlehem the town of David, because he belonged to the house and line of David. He went there to register with Mary, who was pledged to be married to him and was expecting a child. While they were there, the time came for the baby to be born, and she gave birth to her firstborn, a son. She wrapped him in cloths and placed him in a manger, because there was no room for them in the inn. (Luke 2.1,3-7)

Song 2: Busy at Christmas

Action on stage as in Version 1 (see page 7). Omit the line of dialogue between Verses 4 and 5. A small group from the choir should sing the part of the 'Family'.

Reader 1 To us a child is born, to us a son is given, and the government will be upon his shoulders.

Reader 2 And he will be called:

Reader 1 Wonderful Counsellor!

Reader 2 Mighty God!

Reader 1 Everlasting Father.

Reader 2 Prince of Peace. (Isaiah 9.6)

Reader 1 The angel said to Mary:

Reader 2 'Do not be afraid, you have found favour with God. You will give birth to a son and you are to give him the name Jesus. He will be great and will be called the Son of the Most High God.' (Luke 1.30-32)

Reader 1 Mary treasured up all these things and pondered them in her heart. (Luke 2.19)

Reader 2 And Mary said, 'My soul glorifies the Lord and my Spirit rejoices in God my Saviour.' (Luke 1.46-47)

Reader 1 The true light that gives light to everyone was coming into the world. (John 1.9)

Song 3: Here in the manger

Directions as in Version 1 (see page 9).

Reader 1 There were shepherds living out in the fields nearby, keeping watch over their flocks by night. An angel of the Lord appeared to them, and the glory of the Lord shone around them, and they were terrified. But the angel spoke to them:

Reader 2 'Do not be afraid. I bring you good news of great joy that will be for all the people. Today in the town of David a Saviour has been born to you. He is Christ the Lord. This will be a sign to you: You will find a baby wrapped in cloths and lying in a manger.'

Reader 1 Suddenly, a great company of the heavenly host appeared with the angel, praising God:

Choir 'Glory to God in the highest, and on earth peace to those on whom his favour rests.'

Reader 2 When the angels had left them and gone into heaven, the shepherds spoke to one another:

Reader 2 'Let's go to Bethlehem and see this thing that has happened, which the Lord has told us about.' (Luke 2.8-15)

Song 4: The shepherds' shuffle

Action on stage as in Version 1 (see page 10).

Reader 1 After Jesus was born in Bethlehem in Judea, during the time of King Herod, wise men from the east came to Jerusalem and asked:

Reader 2 'Where is the one who has been born King of the Jews? We saw his star in the east and have come to worship him.'

Reader 1 When King Herod heard this he was disturbed, and all Jerusalem with him.

Reader 2 He called together all the people's chief priests and teachers of the law and spoke to them.

Reader 1 'Where is the Christ to be born?'

Reader 2 'In Bethlehem in Judea, for this is what the prophet has written.'

Reader 1 Then Herod called the Wise Men secretly and found out from them the exact time the star had appeared.

Reader 2 And he sent them to Bethlehem:

Reader 1 'Go and make a careful search for the child. As soon as you find him, report to me, so that I too may go and worship him.'

Reader 2 After they had heard the king, they went on their way, and the star they had seen in the east went ahead of them until it stopped over the place where the child was. When they saw the star, they were overjoyed. (Matthew 2.1-10)

Song 5: March of the wise men

Action as in Version 1 (see page 11).

Reader 1 But having been warned in a dream not to go back to Herod, the wise men returned to their country by another route.

Reader 2 When Herod realised that he had been outwitted by the wise men, he was furious, and he gave orders to kill all the boys in Bethlehem who were two years old and under. (Matthew 2.12, 16)

Reader 1 The light shines in the darkness, but the darkness has not understood it. (John 1.5)

Reader 2 This is the verdict: light has come into the world, but people loved darkness instead of light, because their deeds are evil. (John 3.19)

Reader 1 Jesus said to his disciples, 'If the world hates you, keep in mind that it hated me first.' (John 15.18)

Reader 2 Jesus said: 'In this world you will have trouble. But take heart! I have overcome the world.' (John 16.33)

(Note that in Version 2 it is suggested that Song 6 be omitted.)

7. Herod the terror

Action as in Version 1 (see page 14).

Reader 1 God so loved the world that he gave his one and only Son, that whoever believes in him shall not perish but have eternal life. (John 3.16)

Reader 2 Thanks be to God for his indescribable gift! (2 Corinthians 9.15)

Reader 1 Jesus said: 'Whoever comes to me I will never turn away.' (John 6.37)

Reader 2 Praise the Lord from the earth. Praise the Lord, you mountains and all hills, fruit trees and all cedars.

Reader 1 Praise the Lord, you wild animals and all cattle, small creatures and flying birds.

Reader 2 Kings, princes, young men and maidens, old men and children . . .

Reader 1 Let them praise the name of the Lord. (Psalm 148)

Reader 2 Let everything that has breath praise the Lord! (Psalm 150.6)

Song 8: All of God's creatures can celebrate

Action as in Version 1 (see page 16).

Reader 1 Arise, shine, for your light has come, and the glory of the Lord rises upon you. Nations will come to your light and kings to the brightness of your dawn. (Isaiah 60.1, 3)

Reader 2 The shepherds hurried off and found Mary and Joseph, and the baby, who was lying in the manger. When they had seen him they spread the word concerning what had been told them about this child and all who heard it were amazed at what the shepherds said to them. (Luke 2.16-18)

Reader 1 On coming to the house, the wise men saw the child with his mother Mary, and they bowed down and worshipped him. Then they opened their gifts of gold and of incense and of myrrh. (Matthew 2.11)

Reader 2 Seek the Lord while he may be found; call on him while he is near. (Isaiah 55.6)

Song 9: Come to the stable

In Version 2, the repeat of Verse 1, Verse 5 and the words spoken by the Adult Jesus after Verse 5, should all be omitted. The action on stage for Verses 1-4 should be as in Version 1 (see page 17). In Verse 6 (i.e. the fifth and last verse sung) a small group of children (not in costume) should join the tableau and kneel in worship at the manger. Of course, the appearance of Uncle Z in the final verse does not occur in this version.

Reader 1 In the past God spoke to our forefathers through the prophets at many times and in various ways, but in these last days he has spoken to us by his Son, whom he appointed heir of all things, and through whom he made the universe. (Hebrews 1.1-2)

Reader 2 The Word became flesh and made his dwelling among us. We have seen his glory, the glory of the One and Only, who came from the Father, full of grace and truth. (John 1.14)

Reader 1 For God who said, 'Let light shine out of darkness,' made his light shine in our hearts to give us the light of the knowledge of the glory of God in the face of Christ. (2 Corinthians 4.6)

Reader 2 Great is the Lord and most worthy of praise!

Reader 1 One generation will commend his works to another. They will tell of his mighty acts. They will speak of the glorious splendour of his majesty. They will tell of the power of his awesome works.

Reader 2 They will celebrate his abundant goodness! (Psalm 145.3-7)

Song 10: If we had a bell

This is presented as in Version 1 (see page 19) by the entire cast on stage plus the choir.

Version 3

It is quite feasible to present the songs and Bible readings as given in Version 2, without any acting at all. Various members and groups of the choir can be arranged to sing the contributions intended for census officers, Mary, shepherds, wise men, Herod, and so on. This version would be particularly appropriate for a church singing group wishing to use the material provided here without involving a large number of children in costume.

1. Silently down to this world

qui - et - ly, sur - pris - ing - ly, the way of God is clear. Gen - tly to this world be - low to take a - way all fear, soft - ly, the prince of peace,

Link between verses and Coda

Je - sus, draws near. Ah

2. Busy at Christmas

Census Officers, Citizens, Family and Choir

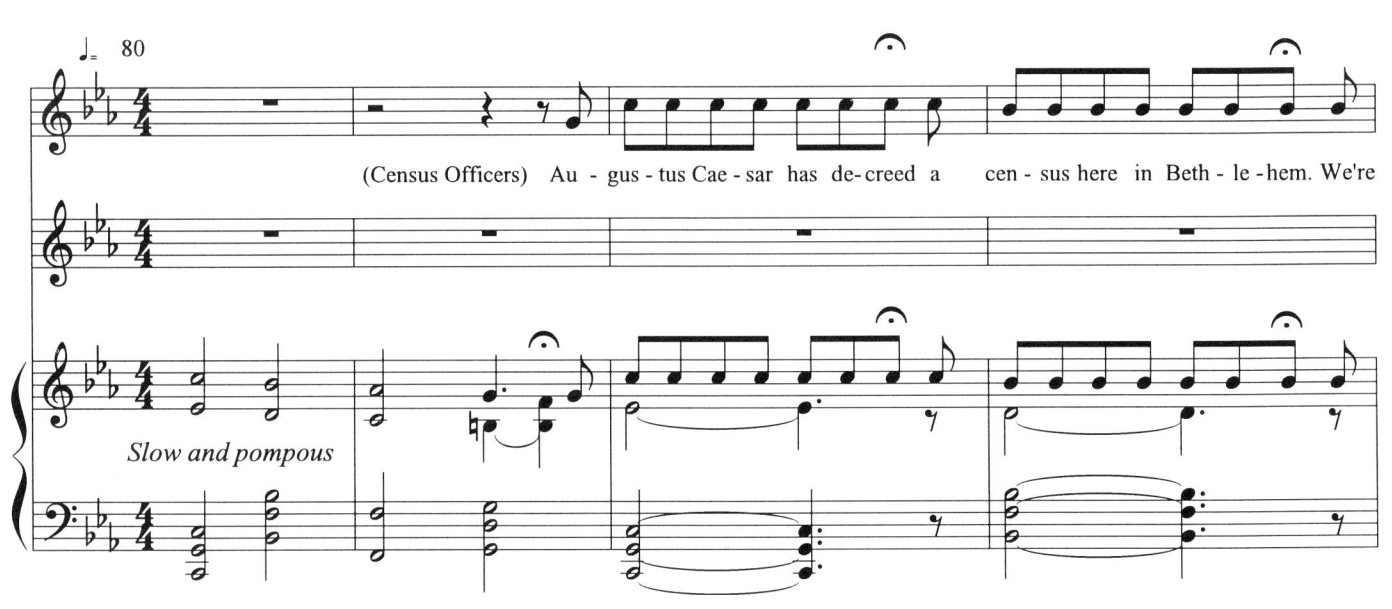

(Census Officers) Au - gus - tus Cae - sar has de - creed a cen - sus here in Beth - le - hem. We're

Slow and pompous

3. Here in the manger

31

4. The shepherds' shuffle

Shepherds
♩ = 80

1. Now we are humble shepherds from the hills up there we come; we do not get much to shout about, our lives are quite hum-drum. It would take a lot our imperturba-
2. A thousand angels, shining bright, announced the Saviour's birth, singing, 'Glory be to God on high and peace to us on earth.' So, then, how could we respond to such a
3. The angel said we'd find him in a stable here about, so we've now arrived in Bethlehem to check the story out. If we find the baby nothing then our

5. March of the wise men

17 frank-in-cense and myrrh they bring, as an off-'ring to the new-born king!

21 2. He's the one the star is point-ing to, he's the anc-ient prom-ise now come true.

25 We are con-fi-dent of this one thing: that this ba-by is the new born king!

29 He's the one the star is poin-ting to, he's the anc-ient prom-ise now come true.

(Choir A)

We are con-fi-dent of this one thing: that this ba-by is the new-born king! 3. Here they come the fa-mous three wise men; they are on their way to Beth-le-hem. Gold and

(Choir B)

3. Here they come the fa-mous three wise men; they are on their way to Beth-le-hem.

frank-in-cense and myrrh they bring, as an off-'ring to the new-born king! He's the

Gold and frank-in-cense and myrrh they bring, as an off-'ring to the new-born king!

He's the one the star is point-ing to, he's the anc-ient prom-ise now come true.

one the star is point-ing to, he's the anc-ient prom-ise now come true. We are

We are con-fi-dent of this one thing: that this ba-by is the new-born king!

con-fi-dent of this one thing: that this ba-by is the new-born king!

6. High on a hillside

Choir
♩ = 88

1. High on a hill-side Je-sus is preach-ing, crowds ga-ther round him, at-tend-ing his word. Those who are wise will res-pond to his teach-ing:
2. High on a hill-side Je-sus is pray-ing, round him his glo-ry shines bright as the day. Then from the hea-vens we hear some-one say-ing:
3. High on a hill-side Je-sus is dy-ing, sin-less one, suff-'ring for wrongs we have done. 'Now it is fin-ished,' tri-umph-ant-ly cry-ing!

'Seek first the king-dom of God.' Thank you, Lord Je-sus, for climb-ing that hill,
'This is my son, him o-bey.'
Vic-t'ry o'er death he has won.

thank you, Lord Je-sus, for do-ing God's will. Glo-ry to God, sing his prais-es for send-ing

Je-sus, his Son. 4. High on a hill-side,

Je-sus asc-end-ing, ri-sen Lord bid-ding fare-well to his friends. Then from his glo-ry his

spi - rit he's send - ing, un - til he comes back a - gain.

(Descant)
Ah — Ah — Ah — Ah — Ah —

Thank you, Lord Je - sus, for climb-ing that hill, thank you, Lord Je - sus, for do-ing God's will.

Glo - ry to God, sing his prais - es for send-ing Je - sus, his Son.

Glo - ry to God, sing his prais - es for send-ing Je - sus, his Son.

7. Herod the terror

Herod and Choir

Very slow and dramatic ♩= 56

Ev - 'ry - one look out! Trou - ble is a - bout! When He - rod cur - ses and blas - phemes, let all be - ware his e - vil schemes. Look out!

1. (Herod) I'm He - rod, the ter - ror, and all the powers of dark - ness are
2. (Herod) I'm He - rod, the ter - ror, I'm caus - ing ut - ter may - hem, dis -

poco piu mosso

gradually getting faster

11 fo-cus-ing on Beth-le-hem to - night. I'm
tress and pain my cru-el plan will bring. My

14 jea-lous of Je - sus, I'm ruth-less and I'm heart-less, I'll do my best to ter-min-ate the
for - ces are search-ing for in-fant boys to slay them, de-ter-mined to des-troy this new-born

17 light.   (Choir) He's He - rod, the ter - ror, and
king.   (Choir) He's He - rod, the ter - ror, he's

marcato

♩= 100

20 all the powers of dark-ness are fo-cus-ing on Beth-le-hem to - night.
caus-ing ut-ter may-hem, dis-tress and pain his cru-el plan will bring.

He's jealous of Jesus, he's ruthless and he's heartless, he'll do his best to terminate the light. The light of the world is Jesus, perfectly holy and true, righteousness shines from his presence, with

His forces are searching for infant boys to slay them, determined to destroy this new-born king. The king of all kings is Jesus, noble and worthy is he. He is the truth sent from heaven, with

power to make all things new. But e - vil op - pos - es good-
power and au - thor - i - ty. Now false - hood and cruel in - jus -

ness, for wrong can - not stand with right.
tice with jus - tice and truth con - tend.

Hat - red strives with the love of God, and dark - ness scorns the light.
But the power of the love of God must tri - umph in the end.

1. Look
2. Must

rit

triumph in the end. Must triumph in the end.

rit. *allargando* *a tempo*

(Herod screams!)

fff

8. All of God's creatures can celebrate

Donkey, Hen, Camel, Cow, Choir

With swing ♩ = 112

1. (Donkey) Now I may be an ass with a face like a clown, I may be the stubborn-est creature in town, and I'll have to concede that my brain is not great, but even a donkey can
2. (Hen) Now I'm only a hen and I live in this shed, and that little child is asleep in my bed! I may only produce the boiled egg on your plate, but even a chicken can
3. (Camel) Now I am an old camel and I know my place. If you think you're ugly take a look at my face. I am simply a beast designed to carry a weight, but even a camel can

CHOIR

cel - e - brate! E - ven a don - key can cel - e - brate!
cel - e - brate! E - ven a chic - ken can cel - e - brate!
cel - e - brate! E - ven a ca - mel can cel - e - brate!

Cel - e - brate! Cel - e - brate! The par - ty's be - gun! All of God's crea - tures can join in the fun! So who - e - ver you are, step right in through the door, he wel - comes the rich and he wel - comes the poor, the high and the migh - ty, the low - ly in state: all of God's crea - tures can cel - e - brate! All of God's crea - tures can cel - e - brate!

4. (Cow) I am on - ly a beast with a

47

diet of grass, I'm not very bright and I'm real working class. I've been stuck in the cow shed and that's why I'm late: *(Speaking) I had udder business to attend to.* But even the cattle can

(CHOIR)
celebrate! Even the cattle can celebrate! Celebrate! Celebrate! The party's begun! All of God's creatures can join in the fun! So whoever you are step right in through the door, he welcomes the rich and he welcomes the poor, the high and the mighty, the lowly in state: all of God's creatures can celebrate!

All of God's crea-tures can cel - e - brate! All of God's crea-tures can cel - e - brate!

molto rit   *a tempo*

9. Come to the stable

Choir and all the cast; one verse solo

♩ = 104

1. Now in your heart, you can come to Beth-le-hem,
2. Down from the hills, shep-herds come to Beth-le-hem,
3. Far from the East, wise men come to Beth-le-hem,
4. All in this world, you can come to Beth-le-hem,

to the sta-ble, to wor-ship God the son. Come now to him, just be-lieve, in faith draw near, his love re-ceive.

From heaven's glo-ry he laid a-side his ro-yal crown, humbled him-self and for our sal-va-tion stepped right down.

You heard the an-gels an-nounce the prom-ised sa-viour's birth, sing-ing of glo-ry to God and peace for those on earth.

Fol-low the star which re-vealed the cho-sen time and place, where God's an-oin-ted des-cends to save the hu-man race.

He left his rich-es of heav'n our po-ver-ty to share, en-tered our world to es-tab-lish heav-en's king-dom here.

Lyrics (m. 29–36):

- So you can come to the stable, a place is for you set a-part:
- So, shep-herds, come to the sta-ble, a place is for you set a-part:
- So, wise men, come to the sta-ble, a place is for you set a-part:
- So, you can come to the sta-ble, a place is for you set a-part:

but will he find a place with-in your heart?
but will he find a place with-in your heart?
but will he find a place with-in your heart?
but will he find a place with-in your heart?

dim ... *rit* ... *a tempo*

After Verse 4 repeat Verse 1

5. (Repeat of Verse 1)

place with-in your heart?

rall ... *mp a tempo*

mf

(Solo)
5. O-pen your eyes, look up high, there on a cross see the one son of God who was born to die.
6. Now in your heart, you can come to Beth-le-hem, to the sta-ble, to wor-ship God the son.

Look up to him, just be-lieve, in faith draw near, new life re-ceive.
Come now to him, just be-lieve, in faith draw near, new life re-ceive.

(Choir) O-pen your eyes now and see the love of God for you,
He left the rich-es of heav'n our pov-er-ty to share,

cresc

look up to Je - sus the sa - viour, dy - ing there for you.
en - tered our world to es - tab - lish hea - ven's king - dom here.

ff

He of - fers life by his death, it's for you that he suf - fers and dies.
So you can come to the sta - ble, a place is for you set a - part.

Look now to him, be - lieve, and o - pen your eyes!
Will Je - sus find a

dim *rit* *a tempo*

place with - in your heart?

rall *a tempo* *rit*

10. If we had a bell

song: now Je-sus Christ is born our king, ding, dong, ding, dong, ding-a-dong-a- ding.

Bing! Bong! Bing! Bong!

molto rall *a tempo* *mf*

(Unison voices) If we had a drum we'd bash it, crash it, tap it, rap it, bang it, beat it. But we have-n't, so we'll bleat it!

Bom, bom, bom, bom, bom, bom, bom, bo- rra bom, bom, bom, bom, bom, bom, bom, bom, bom, bom, bom, bom, borr-a-borr-a- bom.

poco rall *a tempo* *mf*

If we had a harp, we'd twang it, clang it, pluck it, strum it, fin-ger and thumb it.

But we have-n't so we'll hum it!

(Choir humming in 4 parts)

poco rall — *a tempo* — *mf*

(Unison voices) If we had a horn, trom-bone or trum-pet, we'd raise it, sound it,

57

65 play all a-round it, pump it, prime it, tune it, chime it. But we haven't so we'll mime it!

(Mime playing various brass instruments, and add sound-effects if desired)

70 *ff* ... *poco rall*

76 If we had a card, we'd

a tempo *mf* ... *f*

read it, write it, lick it, bend it, stick it, send it. But we have-n't so pre - tend it: We wish you a mer - ry Christ-mas, we wish you a mer - ry Christ-mas, we wish you a mer - ry Christ-mas and a hap - py new . . . If we were an-gels up in hea-ven, we would praise him, sing hal-le-lu-jah. But we're not, we're here, but we'll still sing it to yer! (groan!) Hal-le-lu-jah! Hal-le-lu-jah! Hal-le-lu-jah! Hal-le-lu-jah! Now

112 we have-n't got a bell to bang it, clang it, bong it, dong it, ring-a-ding-a-ding it,

poco piu mosso
pp *cresc poco a poco*

117 have-n't got a drum to bash it, crash it, tap it, rap it, bang it, beat it,

mp

121 have-n't got a harp to twang it clang it, pluck it, strum it fin-ger and thumb it

mf

haven't got a horn, trombone or trumpet, to raise it, sound it, play all around it,

pump it, prime it, tune it, chime it, haven't got a card to read it, write it,

lick it, bend it, stick it send it, so we'll join with the angels up in heaven

meno mosso

sing his prais - es, shout hal - le - lu - jah! Glo - ry now to God we sing, give

poco rall

thanks for Je - sus born our king, re - joice in praise be - fore him. O

come let us a - dore him, Christ ____ the Lord!

molto rall

Related titles from National Society/Church House Publishing

Mother Teresa
a musical
Peter Churchill

An unusual musical tracing the life of one of the best-loved Christians of the twentieth century. The eleven songs range from a beautiful setting of Mother Teresa's famous prayer 'Make me worthy, Lord' to a chorus of singing and dancing nuns.

Ideal for performance in church or as a school musical, a full performance lasts around 45 minutes.

***Full Music Edition*: £7.95   *Words Only Edition* pack of 10: £7.50**

Plays on the Word
Derek Haylock

A collection of nineteen humorous drama sketches (including eight for Christmas) ideal for family services, school assemblies or church drama groups. All firmly Bible-based, topics range from a TV newscast report of the Crucifixion and Resurrection to a challenge to Christmas-only churchgoers.

The book's brilliant!
A CHURCH DRAMA GROUP LEADER

£5.95

Sketches from Scripture
Derek Haylock

Twelve more fast-moving, entertaining sketches designed for performance with a minimum of rehearsal. There are sketches to make you laugh ... and to make you think, including *The Prodigal Daughter* (a new twist to the familiar story), *A Grave Business* (the story of the raising of Lazarus) and *The Last of These* (focusing on the needs of children worldwide).

£4.95

THE NATIONAL SOCIETY
A Christian Voice in Education

The National Society (Church of England) for Promoting Religious Education is a charity which supports all those involved in Christian education – teachers and school governors, students and parents, clergy and lay people – with the resources of its RE Centres, archives, courses and conferences.

Founded in 1811, the Society was chiefly responsible for setting up the nationwide network of Church schools in England and Wales and still provides grants for building projects and legal and administrative advice for headteachers and governors. It now publishes a wide range of books, pamphlets and audio-visual items, and two magazines, *Crosscurrent* and *Together*.

For details of membership of the Society or to receive a copy of our current catalogue please contact:

> The Promotions Secretary,
> The National Society,
> Church House,
> Great Smith Street,
> London
> SW1P 3NZ
> Tel: 071-222 1672